A family from
BRAZIL

Julia Waterlow

RSVP
RAINTREE
STECK-VAUGHN
P U B L I S H E R S
The Steck-Vaughn Company

Austin, Texas

FAMILIES AROUND THE WORLD

A family from **BOSNIA**

A family from **BRAZIL**

A family from **CHINA**

A family from **ETHIOPIA**

A family from **GERMANY**

A family from **GUATEMALA**

A family from **IRAQ**

A family from **JAPAN**

A family from **SOUTH AFRICA**

A family from **VIETNAM**

The family featured in this book is an average Brazilian family. The De Goes family was chosen because it was typical of the majority of Brazilian families in terms of income, housing, number of children, and lifestyle.

Cover: The De Goes family outside its home with all its possessions
Title page: The De Goes family
Contents page: Children in the local playground

Picture Acknowledgments: All the photographs in this book were taken by Peter Ginter. The photographs were supplied by Material World/Impact Photos and were first published by Sierra Club Books in 1994 © Copyright Peter Ginter/Material World. The map artwork on page 4 is produced by Peter Bull.

© Copyright 1998, text, Steck-Vaughn Company

Published by Raintree Steck-Vaughn Publishers, an imprint of Steck-Vaughn Company

Printed in Italy. Bound in the United States.
1 2 3 4 5 6 7 8 9 0 02 01 00 99 98

Library of Congress Cataloging-in-Publication Data
Waterlow, Julia.
A family from Brazil / Julia Waterlow.
p. cm.—(Families around the world)
Includes bibliographical references and index.
Summary: Describes the typical day in the life of a Brazilian family living in São Paulo.
ISBN 0-8172-4910-9
1. Brazil—Social life and customs—Juvenile literature.
2. Family—Brazil—Juvenile literature.
[1.Family life—Brazil. 2. Brazil—Social life and customs.]
I. Title. II. Series: Families around the world.
F2510.W38   1998
306.85'0981—dc21   97-26553

Contents

◈ Introduction

Brazil is in South America. It is the fifth largest country in the world.

BRAZIL

Capital city:	Brasília
Size:	3,286,728 sq. mi. (8,511,970 sq. km)
Number of people:	159,100,000
Language:	Mainly Portuguese
People:	54% European, 38% mixed race, 6% African, 1% Japanese, and 1% Amerindian or other races
Religion:	Mainly Roman Catholic
Currency:	Real

THE DE GOES FAMILY

Size of household:	6 people
Size of home:	1,076 sq. ft. (100 sq. m)
Workweek:	Sebastiao: 60 hours
	Maria: Always busy
Most valued possessions:	Sebastiao: Car
	Maria: Religious statue
	Eric: Cuddly toy
	Ewerton: Plastic gun
Family income:	$4,200 each year

The De Goes family is a typical Brazilian family. The family has put everything that it owns, except its car, outside the home so that this photograph could be taken.

Meet the Family

1. Sebastiao, father, 35
2. Maria, mother, 29
3. Eric, son, 7
4. Ewerton, son, 7

5. Elaine, daughter, 6
6. Priscila, daughter, 6 months

RICH AND POOR

Some of the richest people in the world live in Brazil. They have servants and live in beautiful houses. But many Brazilians are very poor. Some families live in wooden or tin shacks without any water or electricity. Many don't have enough food to eat.

The De Goes family lives in the city of São Paulo. Sebastiao and Maria have four children. The two boys, Eric and Ewerton, are twins. Friends and family often come to visit. The family is not rich, but Sebastiao has a good job, and the family has enough money to live on.

"I love all my children. When baby Priscila cries, I give her a big cuddle and she usually stops."—*Sebastiao*

A Home in São Paulo

The De Goes family has painted its house a bright blue.

Brazil is a huge country. Almost half of it is covered in tropical rain forest. Most of Brazil's people live in cities near the coast. São Paulo is Brazil's largest city, and it is one of the biggest in the world. More than 10 million people live there.

A New House

The front door of the De Goes' house opens on an alley. The children can play in the alley with their friends. No one has to worry about traffic. The house is new, and another one is still being built next door. Most of the family's furniture is modern.

Home Comforts

The house has a living room, a kitchen, two bedrooms, and a tiny bathroom. In the living room there are two comfortable chairs and a color television. Maria loves to listen to music, so the family also has a record player. It is never very cold in São Paulo, so their house doesn't have carpets or central heating.

Maria rests in the living room. In the middle of the day in summer it gets very hot.

A Full Bedroom

The older children share one of the bedrooms. The twins share bunk beds. Elaine has her own bunk bed. Elaine's aunt, Magna, often comes to stay. She usually brings Elaine's cousins with her. Aunt Magna and one of Elaine's cousins sleep in Elaine's bed, and Elaine sleeps on the floor with her other cousins. Elaine doesn't mind—she loves having visitors.

This is the children's bedroom. It is often full of friends and family.

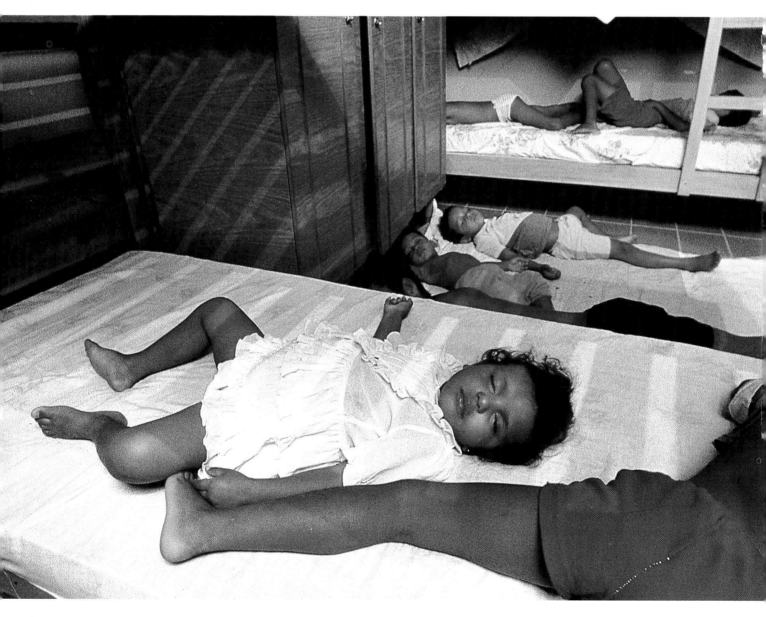

A Flat Roof

The house has a flat roof, which is very useful. Maria can do the washing there. It is also a safe place for the children to play.

Maria does the washing on the roof of the house. In the alley below, children are playing soccer.

 # Food and Cooking

FOOD OF ALL KINDS

Nearly every kind of food is grown in Brazil. The main dish for most people is beans and rice. People who can afford it have meat, and there are delicious fruits of all sorts. Brazil is especially famous for its coffee and sugar.

In the kitchen, the De Goes family has a stove to cook on and a table at which they eat.

A typical meal of beans, rice, and meat

12

Setting the Table

When the family is going to eat, Maria sets the table with a tablecloth and flowers. Usually, only the adults eat at the table because there isn't room for the children as well. The children sometimes take their food into the living room and watch television while they are eating.

Maria's sister, Magna, gives her children lunch in the kitchen. They don't sit at the table because they won't sit still for long!

Shopping

The De Goes family goes shopping once a month to the big supermarket. Maria also visits a local store every day or two to buy bread and milk. The family always has rolls with butter for breakfast. Sebastiao and Maria drink sweet coffee, but the children like chocolate milk.

Maria and Sebastiao pile their carts high with food at the supermarket.

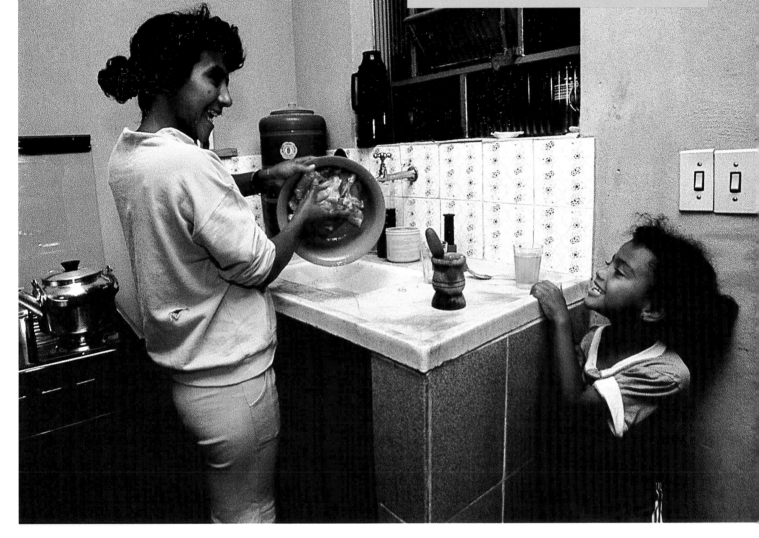

Beans and Rice

Like most Brazilian families, the De Goes eat a lot of beans and rice. They have them nearly every day. Sometimes Maria makes a meat stew to go with the beans and rice and she also cooks fried eggs. The children's favorite meal is meat stew, sausages, and fried eggs.

Working in the City

Maria always puts away the family's clothes in a wardrobe.

Most people in Brazil work in cities. It is difficult to find good jobs. In poor families, children often have to work to help the family make ends meet. Some sell fruit or matches on the street, shine shoes, or clean car windshields.

Clean Clothes

Maria likes her family to wear clean clothes. But this means that she has to do a lot of washing and ironing. The De Goes family has a washing machine, but Maria washes their best clothes by hand.

"My sister sometimes helps me with the washing. We talk so much we forget that we're working."—*Maria*

A Helping Hand

Maria and her friends help each other with their housework from time to time. Maria's friend Enezia often comes to visit Maria and helps her with the ironing.

Maria likes to clean and tidy. Every day she washes the floors, makes the beds, and folds the clothes away. Once a week Maria cleans underneath all the furniture. The pots and pans in the kitchen are always bright and shiny.

Maria sweeps and cleans the house from top to bottom every day.

On the Buses

Sebastiao works as a bus driver in São Paulo. He likes his job, although it takes a long time to drive anywhere in the city because there's so much traffic. He doesn't like starting work at 3:30 A.M., but he gets home early in the afternoon. Maria sometimes works on the buses as well, collecting the money from the passengers.

"I'm always getting stuck in traffic jams— the traffic's terrible in São Paulo."—*Sebastiao*

Play and School

Some of the children's favorite toys

Many families in Brazil have a lot of children. Some of them never learn to read and write. About 5 million children between 7–14 don't go to school at all. Government schools are not always very good. Parents like to send their children to private schools if they have enough money.

Playing Games

Although Eric and Ewerton are twins, they like to do different things. Eric's favorite toy is a fluffy animal that he likes to take to bed with him. Ewerton pretends that he is a gangster with his toy gun. Elaine's favorite toy is her doll.

▲ Elaine and her best friend, Manuella, have fun at the playground.

There are not many parks in São Paulo. If the children want to go outside, they usually play in the alley beside the house. There are lots of other children in the neighborhood to play with. The boys always kick soccer balls around.

"I love chasing Pelé around the washing."— *Rodrigo, the children's cousin.*

▶ Rodrigo sometimes brings his dog, Pelé, to visit his cousins.

Off to the Nursery

The De Goes children go to the nursery during the week. Maria takes them because she doesn't think it is safe for them to go alone. The children spend all day at the nursery. When they come home, the children help Maria around the house. Then she lets them watch television.

The nursery is just a short bus ride from home.

"It's fun being a twin. Sometimes Ewerton pretends to be me at school and our teacher gets mixed up!"—*Eric*

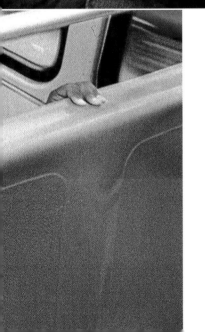

Changing Schools

The boys will start primary school soon. There they will have lessons in math, history, geography, and Portuguese. Maria and Sebastiao can't afford books for the children, so they don't read much at home.

23

Spare Time

The De Goes family watches a lot of television. Maria and Sebastiao also like to listen to music.

Relaxing at Home

The De Goes family usually relaxes with friends at home in their spare time. Maria talks to her sisters and friends and listens to music. Sebastiao's friend, Marcos, often comes to visit. Sometimes, Marcos and Sebastiao sit together in the living room watching television.

On hot evenings, Sebastiao sometimes sits outside in the alley talking to neighbors. None of the family plays much sports, but the boys like to watch car racing, soccer, and cartoons on television.

The Car

Sebastiao loads the car
with shopping at the
supermarket.

Many people in São Paulo own cars. Some
families even go without food to pay for them.
The De Goes family is very proud of its car. Maria
and Sebastiao use all their spare money to pay
for it. Sebastiao drives the car to work every day.

Sunday is the family's main day off. Maria likes
to go to church. The family does not go away on
vacation, but they sometimes have a day out.
One of their favorite places is the seaside near
São Paulo. The children love to swim and play
in the sand.

"I don't go to church every Sunday, but I keep some religious things at home."—*Maria*

Living for Today

SHARING BRAZIL'S RICHES

Brazil is rich in many ways. It has rivers, forests, and useful minerals. Brazil's farms produce plenty of food. But many of the people there are poor. They need houses, jobs, schools, and health care. It is hoped they will have a bigger share of Brazil's riches in the future.

Sebastiao and Maria don't spend a lot of time thinking about the future. They enjoy what they have now. They want the children to do well at school and get good jobs when they are older. Maria hopes the children will have families of their own one day.

Maria buys some cakes as a treat for the children.

"I just want everyone to be happy!"—*Eric*

Pronunciation Guide

Carnaval	Car-nah-vahl	**real**	ray-ahl
		Rodrigo	Rod-ree-goo
De Goes	Day-Goh-ez		
		São Paulo	Sawn Pah-ow-lah
Enezia	Eh-nees-see-uh	**Sebastião**	Seh-bahs-tee-own
Ewerton	You-wer-tone		
Marcos	Mar-kohs		
Manuella	Mahn-way-lah		
Pelé	Peh-lay		
Priscila	Pree-see-lah		

Glossary

Amerindians People who lived in South America before Europeans arrived.

Carnaval A week every year when everyone in Brazil likes to have fun. They dance, sing, and dress up in colorful clothes.

Celebration A special occasion when people enjoy themselves.

Costumes Clothes that people wear for fun.

Elections When people vote to choose their leaders.

Independent Able to make your own decisions about what to do.

Minerals Metals and chemicals. They are found in the ground and water around us.

Parades Shows that move along the streets in front of watching crowds.

Rain forest Thick forest that grows in parts of the world where it is hot and rainy.

Shacks Roughly built huts or cabins.

Books to Read

Bailey, Donna and Anna Sproule. *Brazil* (Where We Live). Austin, TX: Raintree Steck-Vaughn, 1990.

Cobb, Vicki. *This Place Is Wet* (Imagine Living Here). New York: Walker & Co., 1989.

Lewington, Anna. *Antonio's Rain Forest*. Minneapolis, MN: Carolhoda Books, 1993.

———— and Edward Parker. *Brazil* (Economically Developing Countries). Austin, TX: Thomson Learning, 1995.

Morrison, Marion. *Brazil: City and Village Life* (Country Insights). Austin, TX: Raintree Steck-Vaughn, 1997.

Index